DAY OF THE DEAD

COLORING BOOK

THUNDER BAY
P·R·E·S·S

San Diego, California

Thunder Bay Press

An imprint of Printers Row Publishing Group
10350 Barnes Canyon Road, Suite 100
San Diego, CA 92121
www.thunderbaybooks.com

Copyright © 2016 Octopus Publishing Group

Printers Row Publishing Group is a division of
Readerlink Distribution Services, LLC.
The Thunder Bay Press name and logo are
trademarks of Readerlink Distribution Services, LLC.

All notations of errors or omissions should be
addressed to Thunder Bay Press, Editorial
Department, at the above address. All other
correspondence (author inquiries, permissions)
concerning the content of this book should be
addressed to Bounty Books, a division of
Octopus Publishing Group
Carmelite House 50 Victoria Embankment
London EC4Y 0DZ
www.octopusbooks.co.uk

An Hachette UK company

Publisher: Peter Norton
Publishing Team: Lori Asbury, Ana Parker,
Laura Vignale
Editorial Team: JoAnn Padgett, Melinda Allman,
Dan Mansfield

ISBN: 978-1-62686-778-9

Printed in China

20 19 18 17 16 2 3 4 5

WELCOME TO THE DAY OF THE DEAD

The Day of the Dead is a Mexican festival held at the beginning of November, a two-day event to honor loved ones who have passed away. It is a whirlwind of color; from beautiful altars decorated with candles, flowers, and fruits, to glittering sugar skulls, intricately painted faces, and guitar-playing skeletons.

Immerse yourself in this cultural phenomenon that has spread across the world, and color in the patterns while letting your imagination roam. Coloring is the perfect way to escape from the frantic pace of everyday life, and the *Day of the Dead Coloring Book* will provide your mind with some welcome relief. Watch this vibrant festival come to life at your fingertips as you pick up your pencils and get to work. It's time to celebrate...

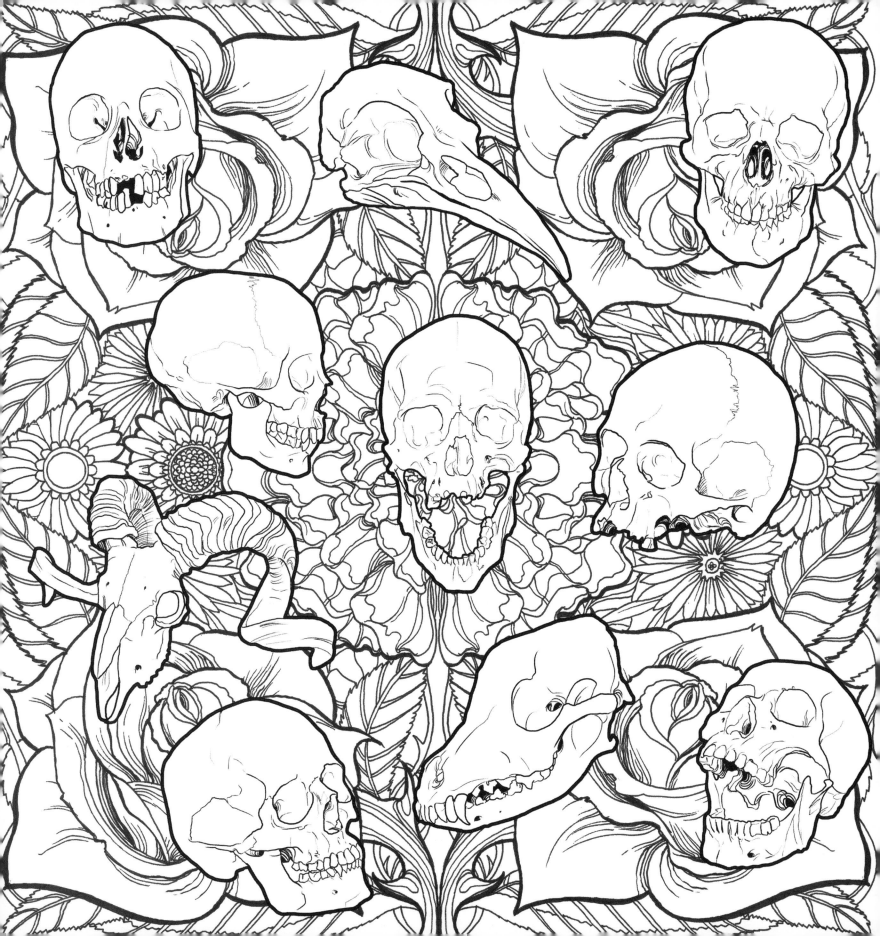

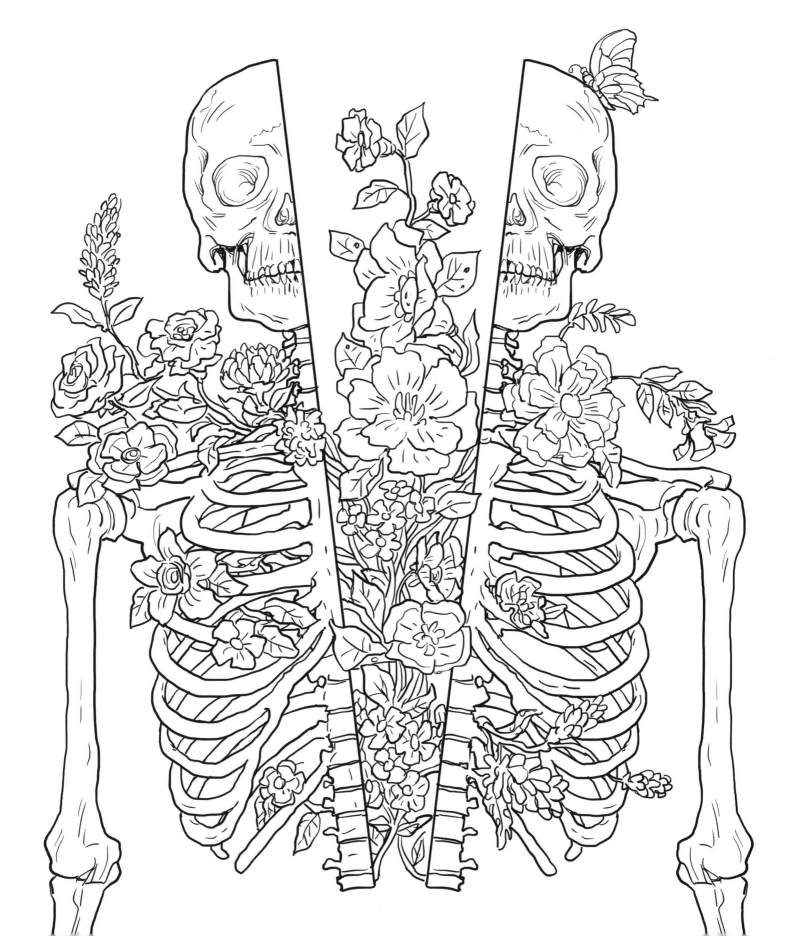

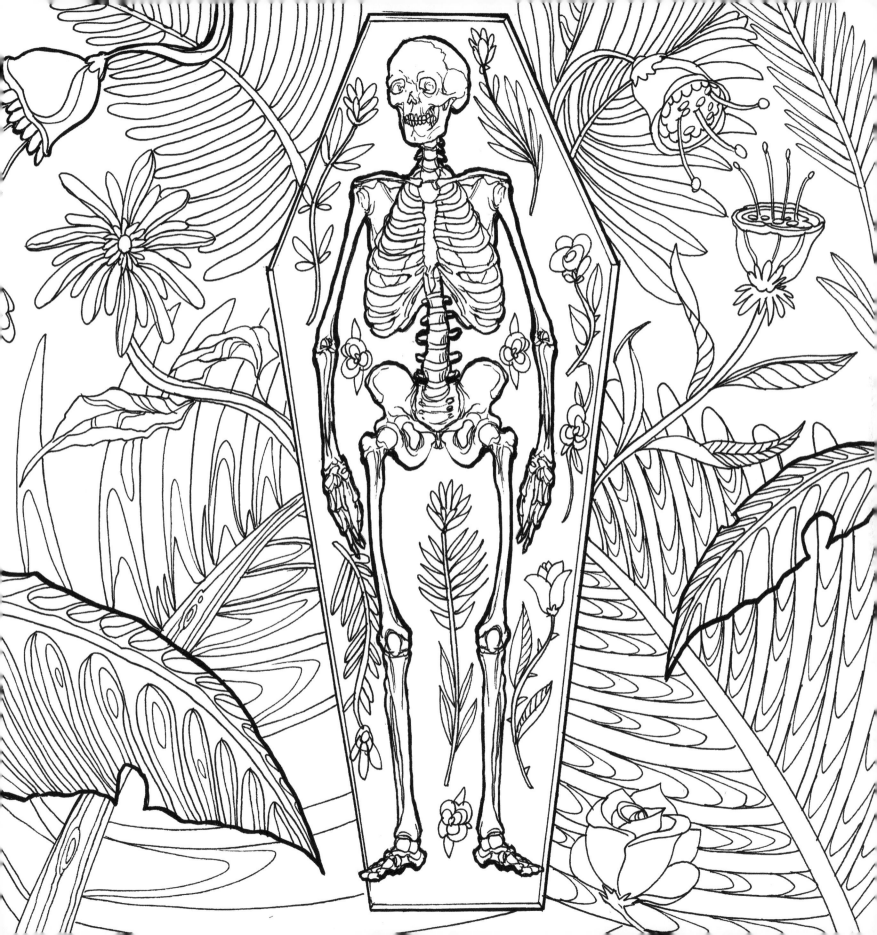

DÍA DE LOS MUERTOS